The Tree of
Beliefs

*Consciously Create Your
Experience by Transforming Your
Mind From the Bottom Up*

Jo-Ellen Fico

The content of this book is published for educational and informational purposes only. The author of this book does not dispense medical advice or prescribe the use of any technique as a form of treatment for physical, mental, emotional, or psychological problems without the advice of a physician. If you are currently being treated by a medical professional for any physical, mental, emotional, or psychological condition, consult with that practitioner prior to modifying any treatment program. In the event you use any of the information in this book, the author and the publisher assume no responsibility for your actions. No express or implied guarantee of results is made.

DEDICATION

To all free thinkers who were ridiculed, rejected, and condemned by imprisoned minds.

Prologue   **6**

Chapter One: Basic Tree of Beliefs   **9**

Chapter Two: Old Paradigm   **16**

     1. Root System   18

     2. Trunk   19

     3. Branches and leaves   20

Chapter Three: New Paradigm   **26**

     1. Root System   28

     2. Trunk   31

     3. Branches and leaves   32

Chapter Four: Missing Links   **46**

Chapter Five: Helpful Tips   **53**

Epilogue   **58**

ABOUT THE AUTHOR   **63**

Prologue

This book is the result of a quest for clarity around questions such as How does life really work? What the heck is going on here? Is personal power an illusion? How can I live without fear? and Is it possible to be happy? These questions, and other related curiosities, ignited in me a ravenous obsession with finding workable answers to unresolved perplexities that seemed to have a life of their own within me. Something demanded answers and this "something," this urge, would not subside until there were clear and non-conflicting conclusions which were applicable and repeatedly provable in my experience. This burning curiosity prompted me to research countless theologies, philosophies, spiritualities, psychologies, and sciences, and to apply them through trial and error in my life. I combined this research and application with frequent observation of myself and others; an observation of experiences, behaviors, relationships, and especially of patterns within them. This led me to eventually glean the essential aspects and applications of various teachings, and to come up with a simple, clear, and user-friendly presentation of a workable model of reality. This model is meant to offer a *concise distillation* of the nature of reality, the nature of the self, and the relationship between them, and to offer a template for the conscious creation of one's life experience. Further, the information herein is intended to assist in promoting a major paradigm shift in thinking. While it incorporates ideas from quantum theory, neuroscience, ancient spiritualities, modern new thought teachings, and information from many other sources, it is not meant to be a comprehensive discourse on any of them. I share here what I found to be the *essentials*, the understanding of which contributed to remarkable positive changes in my own life. I am sharing what worked for me.

There were two perplexities in particular that haunted me. One was that different spiritual teachings seemed to provide conflicting answers to life's mysteries. Who was right? Which teaching could I trust? Secondly, I noticed that some people had positive, and even miraculous changes occur for them from the application of certain teachings, while others had little to no positive outcomes from the application of the very same teachings. Why? What were the reasons for the discrepancies in results? Many people are now asking this same "why" question. The one general premise that unites various teachings in the areas of self help and spirituality is that our inner reality creates or influences our outer reality. If this is so, and we have been given the techniques to change our inner thoughts and beliefs in order to positively influence outcomes, then why do so many fail to achieve positive results? Many of us had been practicing positive thinking, law of attraction, new thought, meditation, and "manifestation" techniques for a long time, seeing at best, mixed results. There seemed to be missing links, or some additional information that if known, could foster more reliable outcomes. This little publication attempts to provide those missing links. It is my vision that the information in this book will in some way contribute to a much-needed paradigm upgrade for our culture.

Chapter One: Basic Tree of Beliefs

I call the following simple graphic the Tree of Beliefs (Figure 1):

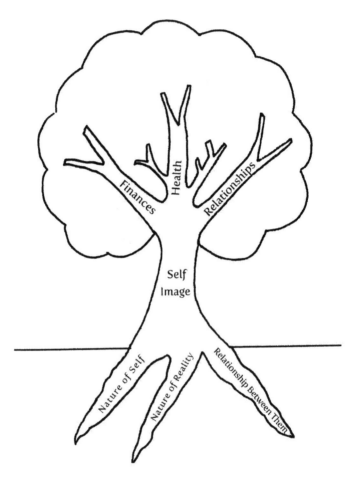

Figure 1

The Tree of Beliefs is a metaphorical representation of a belief system or paradigm that is based on, and grows out of, fundamental beliefs at the root level. The belief systems represented by the Tree of Beliefs in Figure 1 are divided into three general categories:

1. The **root system** comprised of beliefs about the nature of reality, the nature of the self, and the relationship between them.

2. The **trunk** representing beliefs pertaining to our self image or how we view and feel about ourselves.

3. The **branches and leaves** which represent all other beliefs, especially in the areas of finances, health, and relationships.

When contemplating the Tree of Beliefs, one's attention should flow from the bottom up. In other words, the root beliefs are the foundational beliefs in one's thought system. These foundational beliefs are critical in informing all subsequent beliefs and in influencing the experiential outcomes of those beliefs. The beliefs about our self image are assigned to the trunk due its large size in comparison to the size of the branches and leaves. The size of the trunk metaphorically represents the level of influence our beliefs about ourselves exert on the outcomes of our experiences. Our self view has a proportionately large impact on our life experiences. Our beliefs about finances, health, and relationships are represented by three main branches which fan out into many smaller branches and further into leaves. These three pillars...finances, health, and relationships...are areas where positive change is commonly sought. In its entirety, the Tree of Beliefs represents a paradigm in thinking, and the root belief system is the foundational component which forms this paradigm.

The effective use of this Tree of Beliefs depends on acceptance of the premise that our thoughts and beliefs are the primary influencers of our life experiences. I am aware that this premise is not new to many readers, but I hope to provide some missing links that will make the process of upgrading our beliefs easier, and the experiential outcomes of the process more reliable. If we accept the premise that our outer life is a "motion picture" representation of our inwardly held beliefs, then we would naturally want to discard beliefs that outpicture as lack, limitation, and disease, and upgrade our thought system to produce positive outcomes. Habitually held thoughts and beliefs become subconscious programs which run on autopilot. These subconsciously held programs have a default setting and operate much like a thermostat does, automatically bringing the organism back to its preprogrammed position. The brain cooperates in maintaining the status quo of the unconscious programming by laying down habituated neural pathways that foster habitual patterns of feeling and behaving which in turn then reinforce the conditioned thinking. This book does not address how the unconscious beliefs got programmed into the mind whether from culture, past lives, childhood conditioning, or traumatic events. It only concerns itself with undoing them. In this approach it doesn't matter how they got in there, only that they are in there, and that they need to be upgraded.

If these beliefs start out as subconscious, or out of conscious awareness, then the obvious first step is to make them conscious, or to become aware of them. This can be done through self observation and self inquiry. In self observation we become aware of our thoughts and feelings, and we observe our speech and behaviors. Our feelings are primarily precipitated by our thoughts and beliefs, so if we notice a negative emotion we just follow it back to its precipitating thought or belief. For example, if I am feeling depressed, I might discover that I believe I am powerless. If I believe I am powerless, this causes me to feel depressed. Believing I am powerless is a very limiting belief. Our speech is much like an ongoing verbal affirmation of our beliefs. Become conscious of your speech, including your inner self talk, and your thoughts and beliefs will be practically spelled out for you. Recently, a friend said to me "Having more money means having more problems." This verbal statement is not a fact but it reveals the limiting belief that he thinks is true. Observe your behaviors and become aware of your motivations because these motivations will give you insight into your beliefs. Pay particular attention to behaviors that are motivated by lack or fear as these behaviors will reveal your limiting beliefs. For example, I engage in people pleasing behavior with my boss because I am fearful that I will lose my job and become homeless. This reveals that I believe in finite supply, that I believe my boss is the source of my supply, and that I believe that the way to assure my supply is to control and manipulate people and circumstances. All of these beliefs are erroneous and limited. In the self inquiry process, one can look within and simply ask oneself questions such as What do I believe about myself? About life? About money? About how to be happy? These processes of self observation and self inquiry are usually quite effective for uncovering hidden beliefs. However, there are certain foundational assumptions which dominate current world culture to such a degree that many people overlook these beliefs entirely and therefore never inquire into their lack of validity. These foundational assumptions and beliefs will be addressed in detail shortly.

While making subconscious beliefs conscious is an essential first step, it is the discarding of these beliefs and the programming of new supportive beliefs that is the most significant part of the process of transformation. And that is what's necessary: nothing short of complete transformation of the mind. I have witnessed many people who have become highly aware of their formerly unconscious self-sabotaging beliefs. They mistakenly thought that simply by bringing them into awareness this would be sufficient for their mind's transformation. This is not correct. I have also witnessed those that, in addition to making their unconscious beliefs conscious, applied themselves diligently to practices for upgrading their belief systems in order to produce supportive outcomes, only to find that even with significant practice and application, there were little or no lasting positive changes. I include myself in this latter group, and these disappointing results were partially responsible for the burning motivation I felt to find reliable answers. Our goal is to experience a complete paradigm upgrade, and we will begin by first understanding the limitations of the old paradigm.

Chapter Two: Old Paradigm

The belief systems of the **old paradigm** are represented in the Tree of Beliefs as follows (Figure 2):

Middle Root: Nature of Reality is Finite Material Universe

Left Root: Nature of Self is Body, Thoughts, Feelings, Personality

Right Root: Relationship Between Them is Mutually Exclusive

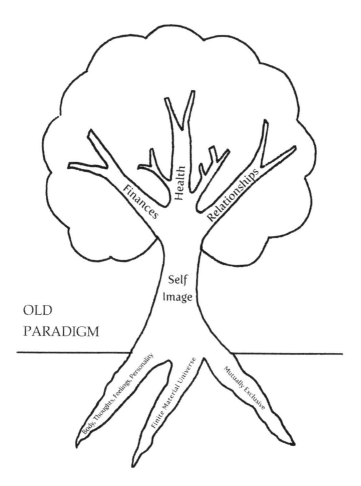

Figure 2

1. Root System

1. <u>Middle Root/Nature of Reality/Independently Existing Material Universe</u>: There is an independently existing material world apart from me which is made of solid and static matter. It is finite and limited. The way this world can be manipulated is by behaviors, actions, and other objectively existing forces, though the material world doesn't always respond reliably to these methods of change. Reality is that which can be verified through the five senses. (What you see is what you get.)

2. <u>Left Root/Nature of Self/Body with Thoughts, Feelings, and a Personality</u>: I am an independently existing object in the world. My identity is primarily that of a body made of matter, though there are also thoughts, feelings and a personality that go into the make up of what I am. I am a tiny fragment in a great big universe, and as such I often feel powerless and fearful. My five senses are reliable witnesses of "what is." I rely on them to inform my decisions of what's possible.

3. <u>Right Root/The Relationship Between Them/Mutually Exclusive/Matter Influencing Matter</u>: I am a subject in an objective world. I am separate from everything and everyone. I am at the mercy of the world and as such I am often victimized by it. It is extremely difficult, and requires a lot of effort for me to effect change in the world or in my circumstances. My options are limited. Change is brought about by myself as matter acting on the objective world of matter; matter influencing matter. My internal world of thoughts and feelings have no relationship to my outer life experiences. Mind and matter are mutually exclusive.

Generally speaking, the above root belief system proffers the idea that there is an independently existing material universe that is apart from me, and that I am an isolated fragment in this universe. The relationship between myself and the universe is mutually exclusive. The means by which I might possibly effect change in my world is through outside forces, though this is an undependable means for transformation with erratic results. The world acts on me and causes my circumstances and my feelings. This overall view of reality and my relationship to it fosters a sense of powerlessness and victimization, causing feelings of fear, anxiety, depression, despair, and hopelessness.

2. Trunk

1. <u>Self Image</u>: My assessment of myself is generally negative. Deep down inside I feel that I am not good enough. I feel somehow deficient. I often feel guilty or shameful. On a core level I don't feel that I am deserving of good things. I base my self image on externals such as my job, my bank account, my accomplishments, my failures, and on others' assessment of me.

3. Branches and leaves

1. **Finances**:

A. <u>Five sense evidence</u>: I can rely on my senses to tell me how much money is available to me. For example, my bank balance or paycheck shows me a finite amount of money and this finite amount is what is available to me. My five sense evidence also tells me that in my culture there are very few ways to get money. For example, getting a job appears to be the most popular way to get money so even though I loathe the idea of a forty hour work week, this seems to be the fate life has to offer if I want to make money. My five sense evidence shows me, for example, that the economy is bad or the housing market is tight and this evidence necessarily limits the opportunities that are available to me.

B. <u>Limited, specific sources</u>: My sources of money are limited and finite. For example, my single source of money is my employer. If I lose my job, I lose my only source of income. Money comes only from specific sources like my ex-husband or the social security administration. Therefore I must do everything in my power to hold on tightly to these specific sources.

C. <u>Finite amounts</u>: This world is made of matter and matter is finite. Resources are finite, and money is definitely finite. There's only so much to go around.

D. <u>Spending mindset</u>: I spend with fear and caution because I don't want to diminish what little I have. I routinely deprive myself.

E. <u>General feeling of lack</u>: I believe that I lack many things. I constantly feel that I don't have enough. I don't have enough money, enough time, enough love in my life. This feeling of scarcity haunts me and as a result I often feel anxious. Lack is my reality.

F. <u>Undeserving</u>: At my core I feel deficient and unworthy. I sometimes feel guilty or ashamed. Deep down inside I don't feel deserving of success or affluence.

2. <u>Health</u>:

A. <u>Material body</u>: My body is made of solid and static matter. The way to effect change in a material body is through material means. The condition of my body is independent of the conditioning in my mind. The condition of my body is not related to my thoughts, my feelings, and my assessment of myself. Only matter influences matter.

B. <u>Material means of healing</u>: Material bodies require material means for healing such as pharmaceuticals and surgeries. I rely on means outside myself for healing. I defer responsibility for my well being and healing to medical professionals.

C. <u>Five sense evidence</u>: Five sense evidence provides me with a diagnosis and it is this that I believe in. I also rely on five sense evidence to inform me of what healing modalities are available to me. For example, if the diagnosis is kidney failure and I hear the doctor tell me that a transplant is my only option, then I have just one possibility for wellness (if I can find a donor in time). This I accept. Further, five sense evidence shows me, for example, that a tumor is growing on my leg and this outside evidence dictates my beliefs. In other words, I do not rule my mind and choose my beliefs; hard, factual, material evidence informs my beliefs about "what is" and what's possible.

D. <u>Limited recourses for healing</u>: My possibilities for healing are limited. After all, there are only two medical treatment options available. Or, there are no possibilities for healing since my condition has been diagnosed as incurable. I do believe my options are limited because I can see only two, or none. Statistics say I have a fifty-fifty chance of survival. I believe in statistics because statistics are hard scientific facts garnered from five sense evidence. Statistics inform my beliefs about what's possible. My beliefs are informed from the outside in.

E. <u>Thoughts and feelings are separate from bodily conditions</u>: My thoughts, feelings, and beliefs are in a domain of their own and are unrelated to the condition of my body. How I feel about myself deep down inside has no effect on the wellness of my body.

E. <u>Unworthiness/self disparagement</u>: Deep down inside I feel that I am unworthy. I judge myself harshly and at times I even feel hatred for myself. At my core I feel somehow deficient.

3. <u>Relationships</u>:

A. <u>I am separate from everyone</u>: My body is separated from all other bodies by space and time. My thoughts are private and have no influence on others.

B. <u>Relationship hierarchies</u>: Some people are more important than others. Some people deserve more respect and consideration than others do. Some people are more powerful than others and can dictate to others how they should think and behave. Some people are the controllers, and the others are the controlled. I am not the sovereign authority of myself.

C. <u>Five sense evidence</u>: My senses tell me that relationship is two or more bodies interacting in space and time. How these bodies come together appears to have no dependable cause; relationships often seem to form randomly. The way I think and feel about myself (the invisible) has no effect on what my relationship experiences are (the visible). What I believe about others has no effect on my relationship outcomes. My senses are reliable in informing me what is possible in relationships. For example, based on what I can see, there are no good men out there.

D. <u>People as sources</u>: Certain people are my source of things such as money, love, and approval. For example, my employer is my source of money, and my girlfriend is my source of love. Since only certain people are my sources, my sources are therefore limited. If I lose my job, I lose my source.

E. <u>Victims and victimizers</u>: In life, people generally fall into one of two categories; victims and victimizers. I am often in the victim category; preyed upon, bullied, disrespected, and harmed by other people. As a victim, I often feel powerless and despairing. Sometimes I feel that I must victimize others in order to get what I need.

F. <u>Unworthiness/deficiency</u>: In my relationships, I often feel like the unworthy party. I feel deficient in comparison to other people.

While all of the above-mentioned examples of beliefs regarding self image, finances, health and relationships may not exactly match your beliefs, the point of including them is to demonstrate how all these beliefs are influenced by one's beliefs at the root level. If the root beliefs are erroneous and limited, most subsequent beliefs will also be limited.

The results of believing in and living by the old paradigm above is a life filled with fear, self judgment, stagnation and a sense of powerlessness and lack. When the self image is negative and fixed this causes repetition of painful patterns, especially in relationships. As a result of adhering to this profitless, upside down thought system we employ coping strategies and compensating behaviors such as self-centeredness, manipulating others to get our needs met, acting out of alignment with our conscience, and in the extreme we resort to substance abuse, crime, and violence. All the ills of the world....mental, emotional, physical, and spiritual...are largely a result of ignorance at the root level (and above) on the Tree of Beliefs.

Chapter Three: New Paradigm

The belief systems of the **new upgraded paradigm** are represented in the Tree of Beliefs as follows (Figure 3):

Middle Root: Nature of Reality is Infinite Field of Potentiality

Left Root: Nature of Self is Sovereign Aware Chooser

Right Root: Relationship Between Them is Correlative/Co-Creative

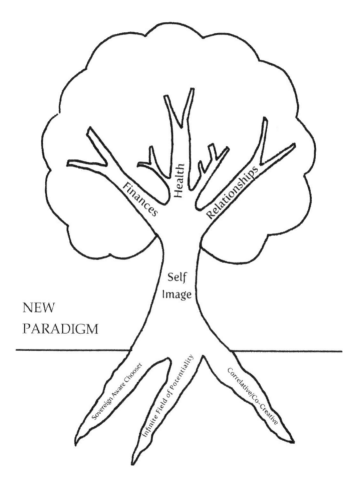

Figure 3

1. Root System

1. <u>Middle Root/Nature of Reality/Infinite Field of Potentiality</u>:

What appears to be a world of solid and static objects which have their own independent, isolated existence apart from the influence of mind is an inaccurate assumption. The universe which is known exists not independently, but in relationship with the knower of that universe. The universe, including bodies, is one boundless interconnected web of energy. That which can be perceived with the five senses, traditionally known as matter, is not actually solid nor static. So called "matter," is actually vibrating energy. This vibrating energy, in various frequencies, is captured by our sense organs and converted by our brain into images, sounds, tastes, sensations, and smells. As such, "matter" is now understood to be much more flexible than previously thought. It is not an immovable solid object, nor is it made of finite substance. Behind that which is perceived with the five senses, traditionally known as matter, exists an invisible, non-finite, unified field of potentiality. This field is the substratum or source of the "material" world. It is a formless, energetic field of pure potentials; infinite probabilities awaiting the focus of our thought to bring specific possibilities into form. This powerful field responds to thoughts and beliefs by intelligently organizing those thoughts and beliefs into particular five sense outcomes or "physical manifestations". (What you think is what you get.) *I keep my focus on the infinite field of potentialities and the energetic nature of the universe and no longer on the material evidence of my five senses.*

2. <u>Left Root/Nature of Self/Sovereign Aware Chooser</u>: My essential self is not an object. My essential nature, that about me which is ever present and unchangeable, is aware beingness which is invisible, boundless, and beyond time and space. Beingness is my intangible sense of existence; the knowingness that "I am" or that I exist. I am self aware, and I am also aware of experiences, sense perceptions, feelings, the body, and especially of thoughts and beliefs. As aware beingness, I possess the will to choose and direct my thoughts and beliefs. Therefore, for practical purposes I know myself as an aware chooser. My thoughts and beliefs, which are also forms of energy, are very powerful and are the influencers of my experiences. As such, my ability to choose my thoughts and beliefs shifts my identity from victim to creator. I am sovereign of my mind because I am a free thinker. I, and I alone, rule my mind. Therefore I am a Sovereign Aware Chooser. My thoughts and beliefs influence the infinite field of potentiality to produce specific outcomes. As such I am a boundless, aware, empowered influencer of the field of possibilities.

3. <u>Right Root/The Relationship Between Them/Correlative and Co-creative/Mind Influencing "Matter"/Energy Influencing Energy</u>: The seemingly separate subject and object (myself as aware beingness and the universe) are actually one wholistic, interactive system. In other words, they are not mutually exclusive. Also, since the universe and an aware chooser and its thoughts share the same essential essence which is energy, they are one in that they are of the same "substance." All seemingly separate objects in the universe are actually a seamlessly connected web of energy. As such, I am connected to everyone and everything, both at the visible level of bodies and things, and at the invisible levels of mind and awareness. I am not at the mercy of the world. I rule my world by ruling my mind. My mind (thoughts and beliefs) and my world are not separate. What seems to be my interior world and the exterior world are in a correlative relationship. Change is brought about by myself as a Sovereign Aware Chooser of thoughts and beliefs influencing the infinite field of potentiality. Aware beingness and the intelligent infinite field of potentiality are co-creators of experience. My internal world of thoughts and beliefs is mirrored in my external life experiences. Mind and matter are interrelated.

Generally speaking, the above root belief system of the new paradigm purports that my inner world and my outer world are correlated. Changes in outer circumstances begin with changes in mind. This paradigm puts me in a position of empowerment as I have dominion over my thoughts and beliefs, and thus over circumstances. This overall view of reality and my relationship to it fosters a sense of upliftment, inspiration, and inner peace.

For practical purposes, and in order for this process to be most efficacious, the essential ideas to take away from the new root paradigm of reality are as follows:

1. The essential nature of reality is an intelligent *Infinite Field of Potentiality*.

2. My essential nature is that of a *Sovereign Aware Chooser* of thoughts and beliefs.

3. The relationship between myself as an aware chooser and the infinite field of potentiality is *correlative*. My self-chosen beliefs influence the field of potentialities in a *co-creative* relationship to produce "material" outcomes.

These ideas must become your new conditioning!

2. Trunk

2. <u>Self Image</u>: My assessment of myself is absolutely positive. Deep down inside I feel that I am a valid, worthy, and complete individual. I know for certain that I have gifts to share. I feel confident and I possess self respect. On a core level I feel that I am deserving of good things.

3. Branches and leaves

1. Finances:

A. Belief in possibilities: I understand that the evidence provided by my five senses is not indicative of what's possible. My focus is on the invisible field of potentialities and not on the material world. I believe in possibilities because I understand that all things that I perceive with my senses have their origin in this field of potentials. What I am now witnessing is just one version of many possible outcomes. I no longer allow what I see to limit my thinking of what's possible. Thought is more powerful than circumstances. Thought transcends matter, the body, space, time and physical laws. Now that I no longer look to externals to dictate what's possible, it is thrilling to contemplate the magnitude and variety of potential outcomes. My attention is focused on potentials!

B. True source of supply: I understand that the true source of all supply is the field of potentiality. This field of potentiality is the substance of all things, including money. I know the energetic substance of this field takes different outward shapes and forms, but at their essence, the shapes and forms are composed of the same basic ingredient. As such, I no longer believe it is difficult to manifest money. There is no longer a compulsion to single out money as something that is more difficult to come by than anything else. The infinite field of potentiality is ever present. It doesn't come and go and it's power does not fluctuate. As such, it is always dependable. I no longer assign or depend on specific persons as my sources of supply. I depend on the faultlessness of the ever present, boundless, intelligent field of potentiality.

C. <u>Supply is not finite</u>: The field of potentiality is not finite, therefore supply is not finite. "Not finite" means having no limits or boundaries. I no longer look to fixed amounts reported to me by my five senses to inform me of what's available. There is an abundance of supply for everyone because the universe is not composed of finite, static matter. It is made of infinite energy. I know I am simply drawing from an inexhaustible supply.

D. <u>Spending mindset</u>: Well-being, beauty, love, generosity, and celebration inform my spending. I understand that fear-based spending sends a belief in lack to the field of potentiality which in turn, produces more lack in my experience. Even though fear-and-lack-based spending is pervasive in current culture, my understanding of the nature of reality and the nature of supply allows me to be strong and to rise above enculturated thinking. I keep my focus on the infinite field of potentials and not on limited dollar amounts. I understand that my behaviors send a message to the field of potentials about what I truly believe, and this includes my spending behaviors. My spending behaviors are based on my belief in possibilities and my understanding of the infinite nature of the source of my supply.

E. General feeling of sufficiency: Because I understand potentiality, and the perpetually present, non-finite nature of this field, I now believe in ever-present sufficiency. I feel that I will always be taken care of.

F. Deserving: At my core, I feel worthy and complete. I like myself and I feel completely deserving of a life of well being, prosperity, and success.

2. Health:

A. Energetic body: My body is actually energy which is vibrating though I cannot perceive this with my five senses. Thus, it is much more malleable than I previously thought. The vibratory rate of my thoughts influences the field of potentiality to produce new outcomes in the vibratory body. Mind influences "matter," which is not actually solid or static.

B. Metaphysical means of healing: My invisible, energetic thoughts, beliefs, and feelings impact the invisible field of potentiality and have an effect on my energetic body. I can improve bodily conditions by taking responsibility for my thoughts.

C. Focus on unseen possibilities: Because I have

knowledge of the infinite field of potentiality, I understand that many potential outcomes are possible, and as such, my focus is on these possibilities and not on the evidence my five senses present to me. Among the many possibilities for healing available to me is the possibility of healing by thought alone.

D. Expanded potential for healing: My beliefs about what is possible are informed by my understanding that a field of infinite potentiality exists behind all sense evidence. Thus, I know the potential for healing exists in spite of any diagnosis.

E. Thoughts and feelings influence bodily conditions: My thoughts, beliefs, and feelings have a direct impact on my bodily conditions. How I feel about myself deep down inside has an effect on the well-being of my body.

F. Worthiness/self respect: Deep down inside I know that I am a worthy individual. At my core I feel complete and fully sufficient. I am confident and have unwavering self respect.

3. Relationships:

A. Everyone and everything is connected: The universe, including bodies and minds, is one unified field of energy in which everything is connected. The connections among minds transcend time and space. Thoughts are part of this interconnected field of energy and as such they influence the entire field.

B. <u>All beings are equal in essence</u>: Our essential nature is unlimited aware beingness. This aware beingness is invisible and is beyond the body, beyond feelings, beyond sense perceptions, and beyond thoughts. It has no variation and is exactly equal in everyone. There are no hierarchies in aware beingness. All beings are equally deserving of sufficiency in all things.

C. <u>Relationships reflect how I feel about myself</u>: Relationships mirror back to me how I view myself. How another treats me is a reflection of how I truly feel about myself. My relationships do not occur randomly. The people in my life represent thoughts and beliefs I hold about myself. The five senses are not reliable witnesses to what's possible in relationships. Relationship possibilities exist first as invisible potentials. I can bring these potentials into my experience by upgrading my beliefs about myself and others. My new beliefs will be reflected either in new relationships or in renewed prior relationships.

D. <u>Field of potentiality as source</u>: The infinite field of potentiality is the source of everything. Specific people are not my sources. Different people may temporarily fulfill a role through which supply can flow to me. These roles are interchangeable and are not limited to specific persons. Further, supply can come through many varied venues, some of which I haven't yet imagined.

E. <u>Empowered sovereign ruler of my mind</u>: Having a victim-consciousness may be pervasive in current culture, but I am a free thinker. I am ruler of my mind and can choose my own thoughts. Being the sovereign ruler of my mind is my true point of power. How I truly feel about myself and my worth determines the dynamics of my relationships. Relationships reflect the beliefs I hold about myself and I am responsible for what I believe. I move from victimization to empowerment by being in charge of the content of my mind.

F. <u>Worthiness/validity/self respect</u>: Deep down inside I feel with conviction that I am a worthy, fully sufficient individual who is deserving of good things. I know I am as valid a being as all others, and I have a high level of self respect.

The above-mentioned beliefs with regard to self image, finances, health and relationships are informed by the upgraded paradigm at the root level. As such, these beliefs are expansive and void of limitation.

The results of believing in and living by the new paradigm above is a life filled with possibilities, inspiration, positive self regard, and a sense of empowerment and sufficiency in all things. When the self image is positive, relationships are harmonious and circumstances are supportive. Coping strategies are no longer needed because of one's dependence on the true source of all supply and the working knowledge of how to tap into it. Behavior is authentic and one lives by the Golden Rule. Peace of mind, generosity of spirit, and celebration are the norm.

By contrast, the consequences of living by the false assumptions of the old paradigm can include mental strain, emotional distress, physical dis-ease, destructive behaviors, and disharmony and lack in one's body of affairs and in the world at large. Most problems can be traced back to a fundamental lack of understanding at the root level. The following lists portray some contrasts in emotion, behavior, and outcomes between living from the old paradigm and from the new:

OLD PARADIGM	NEW PARADIGM
Fear, anxiety	Peace through knowledge
Depression, unhappiness	Peace through mind without limitations
Powerlessness, hopelessness	Empowerment
Grudges, judgment	Forgiveness through understanding
Frustration, anger, struggle	Inspiration
Personas, masks, people pleasing	Authenticity and integrity in interactions
Getting mentality and behavior	Having mentality, giving and sharing
Lack consciousness	Sufficiency consciousness
Low self worth	High self regard
Coping strategies	Knowledge of nature of reality and self
Substance abuse, addiction	Celebration
Me-centered behavior	Golden Rule, highest good of all
Crime, violence	Knowledge of conscious creation

Clinging to people and situations	Knowledge of true source frees others
Stagnation, maintenance of status quo	Change, improvement, expansion
Sickness, fatigue	Well-being, energized
Fear-based spending, deprivation	Celebration, love, generosity inspire spending
Hoarding	Circulating
Manipulation by force	Outer change through inner change
Controlling others	Focus on field, not on controlling people or matter
Relationship hierarchies	All have equal right to sufficiency
Competition, greed	Sufficient supply for all, generosity
Rigidity, routines	Spontaneity, inspiration

The new upgraded paradigm has the capacity to release the mind from worry and fear and to foster feelings of empowerment and inspiration. If you think differently, you feel differently. And if you are also willing to choose to behave differently----to bravely behave in accordance with the new paradigm in thinking----you have a potent recipe for effective conscious creation. Congruence in thought, feeling, and behavior sends a clear, laser-focused, powerful message to the infinite field of potentiality.

****

The primary goal is to make the new root paradigm your new conditioning. All subsequent beliefs are informed by beliefs at the root level. It is much easier to change trunk, branch, and leaf beliefs with knowledge and understanding of the new, upgraded root paradigm. When you understand that the nature of reality is possibilities, then choosing a new belief is simply a matter of choosing a different possibility from a pool of many possibilities. Beliefs *are* possibilities, one as equally easy to exchange as another. You are not focused on trying to change matter at the five sense level, you are simply picking a new possibility from an invisible field of possibilities. With regard to changing beliefs about your self image, for example, someone from your past may have told you that you're not good enough. This is one possible description which reflects their misguided accusation only. This possibility is not a fact. This one possibility doesn't have to be a life sentence. Why limit yourself to one possibility? You *must* understand that beliefs are easily interchangeable, and all possibilities exist in potential in the field of potentiality. Many people spend a lot of time trying to change beliefs at the trunk, branch and leaf levels without first making a paradigm shift at the root level. They say positive affirmations but inwardly they don't believe them. This conflict causes mixed results or no positive change at all because the deep inner beliefs are stronger than the positive affirmations. Many people have a very difficult time convincing themselves that the new belief is true. But if it is understood that beliefs share equal potentiality, and that all beliefs are equally available for the choosing, this conversion over to the new belief is much easier. No belief is intrinsically true. Beliefs become the "truth" of your experience when they are chosen and conditioned in the mind. Beliefs do not dictate what is true. You, as an aware chooser, dictate what will be "true" in your experience by choosing your beliefs. You must understand and know that one belief is as easy to choose as another *because* all possibilities exist in potential in the field. Furthermore, you are not required to be able to see or to figure out how these possibilities will actualize in your experience. The intelligence of the field of potentiality can orchestrate outcomes in ways that you cannot fathom. You mustn't limit your possibilities to only those that you feel that you yourself can figure out how to actualize.

I manifest myself. The concept of "manifesting" is very popular among those who use techniques for the conscious creation of experience. We often hear them say "I am manifesting a new car" or "I manifested a new house" for example. I'd like to suggest a deeper, more wholistic concept of manifesting. It is the idea that I manifest myself. In other words, if you look out at your life---your relationships, your health, your financial situation, etc----you see a "motion picture" representation of your mind, and especially of your self image. This approach can be helpful when attempting to uncover hidden beliefs. Your world is a mirror of your mind. The conditions of your life and the condition of your body point to your deeply held beliefs, especially about yourself. Shifting your thinking over from "I manifest things" to "I manifest myself" can provide a surprisingly helpful new perception. If you consider this new concept, "I manifest myself," and then you look out over your life situation and especially at your relationships, you may have a type of aha experience that you are actually looking at the mirror of what you believe about yourself. Utilizing the concept "I manifest myself" can provide direct access to broad core beliefs which need upgrading.

Another angle to consider when using the "I manifest myself" idea is that in essence, both my inner self and the outer world are energy. Therefore, I manifest what I am, though in a variety of frequencies which match the vibrations of my thoughts and beliefs. Alternatively, one could hold the thought "It's all energy," both inner and outer. Energy influencing energy. Therefore, I manifest myself. Holding the idea that "It's all energy" or that "I manifest myself" rather than thinking that I manifest objects or circumstances can loosen up belief systems, which can make it much easier for the mind to believe in change and possibilities.

Total transformation of the mind. As stated above, the intention is to first transform the mind at the root level from the old paradigm to the new paradigm. It is critical to upgrade our understanding of all three roots: the essential nature of reality (middle root), the essential nature of self (left root), and the relationship between them (right root). We recall that the essential nature of reality is an invisible, malleable, energetic, non-finite field of potentiality, and we as aware choosers influence that field to produce outcomes based on the predominant thoughts and beliefs held in the mind. Of special importance is the updating of our old beliefs about the middle root: the nature of reality. The collective consciousness of current culture believes in a solid, finite, independently exiting universe of matter. Reality according to this paradigm is only what the five senses report. In this belief system, the evidence of the five senses is what's true. Our habitual reliance on sense evidence to inform us of what's possible must be turned on its head. A new habit of reliance on possibilities must be formed. This fundamental reversal is crucial and is the crux of this transformation. Our focus and faith must be on the ever present infinite field of potentialities and its power to intelligently orchestrate outcomes. Then, we may apply our belief in possibilities to our self image, knowing that our identity is not defined by others' assessment of us, by the sense evidence of our current circumstances, nor by our past. Nothing outside of us need define us. We are the sovereign choosers of our positive self view, and we can choose for ourselves from the well of possibilities. Subsequently, we can apply belief in possibilities to specific life circumstances such as believing that there is more than one option for treating my kidney failure, or more than one source of supply than alimony from my ex. Then we can expand our belief in possibilities to broader areas such as overall health or finances in general. The transfer of this new habit of belief in non-finite possibilities then extends to all thoughts and all things. We completely take the lid off of limitations. In other words, we put no limitations whatsoever on thought, belief, or outcome. We free the mind! You may catch yourself from time to time believing in limited possibilities, and it will become quicker and easier to let those limitations go. Once the shift over to the new paradigm has become your new conditioning, affirmations and other reprogramming techniques are generally no longer needed. The mind believes in possibilities and is free of limitations. The intelligent and infinite field of potentiality automatically supplies sufficiency in all things because there are no longer limiting thoughts to impede its fullness. Some people know this as Divine Providence. The mind feels happy when it is aware of its power and is not cluttered with limitations. If a benign desire arises, it is often easily fulfilled without the use of repetitive affirmations. A single thought can be very powerful if it is not diluted and defeated by competing limiting thoughts.

Chapter Four: Missing Links

Below are what I discovered to be the missing links which prevented consistent, positive results from the application of belief-updating practices, and other tools for the conscious creation of one's experience:

1. A paradigm shift at the root level must become your new conditioning! Many people spend a lot of time updating their beliefs at the trunk and branch levels but remain ignorant of the erroneous and limiting beliefs at the root level. Their affirmation and reprogramming efforts do not include their thoughts about the nature of reality. This can cause mixed or meager results. Our thoughts about the nature of reality and our relationship to it influence all subsequent thoughts and beliefs. *It is much easier to change our programming at the trunk and branch* *levels if we first reprogram our minds at the root level.*

2. Understanding the nature of reality (middle root) is essential. Understanding that the essential nature of the universe is an energetic, malleable, non-finite field of potentials is critical for consistent results in the conscious creation of one's experience. One must know that *'possibilities'* is the basic underlying nature of reality. Without this knowledge it is very difficult for one to believe that conditions can change or improve easily or at all. At best, one can see very limited options for change. Without this knowledge people get mixed results when attempting to use the power of thought to effect change in their circumstances or themselves because the mind simply cannot believe in the new thought they are affirming. This sets up a conflict and the old strongly programmed beliefs usually win out. The way to increase belief in possibilities is to understand that the nature of the universe *is* possibilities. The understanding of the nature of reality must shift from that of finite, static matter----- that which is reported by the five senses-----to knowledge of the invisible, intelligent, infinite field of potentiality.

3. The nature of oneself as aware chooser and its relationship to the field of potentiality is key. Knowing that ourselves as sovereign aware choosers and the infinite field of potentiality are in an unceasing correlative relationship is key to success at using the power of belief to effect positive change.

Every moment we are choosing our thoughts and beliefs even when we are not conscious that we are choosing. In other words, our subconscious programming is in ceaseless interaction with the field of potentiality. Those who apply techniques for changing their beliefs in order to improve their circumstances often get meager or mixed results because they haven't sufficiently reprogrammed their subconscious mind. They may be attentive to saying affirmations, doing visualizations, and applying other techniques but the applications were not sufficient to tip the scale over to the new beliefs. Without understanding that they are in *constant* relationship with the field of potentiality, their efforts are too casual. One's mind must be conditioned to the new paradigm that we are not separate from the world; that mind and "matter" are in a non-stop, co-creative relationship. Understanding this new paradigm will show the critical importance of our becoming conscious, sovereign rulers of our minds, and will inspire the commitment necessary for the mind's complete transformation.

4. Behaviors must align with beliefs! If I could write these words in fire blazing across the sky to get your attention, I would. *You must not engage in behaviors which contradict your new beliefs. Your behavior must be congruent with your new beliefs, especially beliefs at the root level.* The behaviors you engage in and the actions you take send a message to the field of potentiality about what you truly believe. In other words, *your behaviors betray your true beliefs*. You cannot choose beliefs from the new paradigm and behave according to the old paradigm and expect positive results. If you choose beliefs from the new paradigm but behave according to the old paradigm you are sending mixed messages to the field of potentiality. These mixed messages will at best cancel each other out, but more likely, the old, more strongly embedded paradigm will predominate and win. Aligning your behavior with your new beliefs is extremely powerful. It sends a congruent message to the field of potentiality. *The failure to align behavior with new beliefs is the number one cause for lack of positive and consistent results* for those who practice new thought/law of attraction/"manifesting" techniques. Such people may consciously choose new beliefs but they are still basing their behavior on evidence from their five senses. This means that at their core they still they believe in the old paradigm. The number one deterrent to aligning behavior with new beliefs is *fear*, especially in the area of money and finances. People find it extremely difficult to make financial decisions based on ever the present and limitless supply from the field of potentiality. The old conditioning around the finite nature of money and supply is so strong. To those who are accustomed to behaving according to the old paradigm because they believe to do so is to ensure survival, behaving according to the new paradigm feels very risky and frightening; it feels as if behaving according to the new paradigm will actually threaten one's survival. If you recondition your mind to the new paradigm at the root level and come to truly understand and to know the energetic, infinite nature of reality and its possibilities, this will eradicate or at least minimize the fear you formerly felt around taking actions that are in alignment with your new beliefs. Taking actions or behaving in alignment with your new beliefs isn't only about taking positive steps towards your goals. It is about no longer engaging in fear-and-scarcity-based behaviors. It is about no longer taking action based on five sense evidence. It is about no longer behaving as if others are your source of supply.

5. One's self image has a proportionately large impact on other beliefs and on all life experiences. How we really feel about ourselves deep down inside, what I call our self image or self view, has a major impact on our life results. In fact, you could say that our outer life is a motion picture of our inner self view. When we feel badly about ourselves, when we view ourselves as unworthy, guilty, or not enough, these self judgments influence all areas of our lives. We attract relationships in which others see us and treat us in correlation to how we see ourselves. These people actually represent our beliefs about ourselves. Our health is directly affected by how we feel about ourselves, whether positive or negative. Our finances are equally affected by our self view. For instance, if we view ourselves essentially as not enough, then other limiting beliefs flow out from that thought such as, "I'm undeserving of success." This belief in turn creates lack of success in business, career, or finances. Many beliefs about relationships, money, and health (branches) grow out of our self view (trunk). Many people make health, finances, and relationships the focus of their affirmations and creation techniques while ignoring their poor self image. This strategy contributes to mixed and meager outcomes. Reprogramming the mind to a positive self view is critical for successful outcomes. Beliefs about one's self image must be upgraded along with beliefs about health, finances, and relationships.

6. Belief in the need to conform to cultural standards must be eradicated! Many people apply belief-updating techniques but they don't take them far enough. They hit a particular ceiling built by current culture which then causes mixed or meager results. Current culture has not come close to tipping the scale over to the new paradigm. The collective consciousness of current culture is operating from the old materialistic, five sense paradigm. This old paradigm is responsible for the current limited ways and means of society. Very often, even though people have expanded their beliefs to some degree, they will hit this ceiling imposed by current culture and feel they must conform to at least some of the ways and means of current culture in order to survive. For example, one limiting concept that is rampant in current culture is the concept of a job as it is commonly structured. It limits available time by imposing a 40 hour work week, it is usually limited to one location such as an office, it often limits creativity, and the single avenue of income is finite in the form of an hourly wage or salary. Even though the job concept may feel excruciatingly confining to the mind and the idea of having money through some other means feels expansive and freeing, because the job concept dominates world culture, fear of poverty and homelessness wells up and induces one to conform both in belief and behavior to the job concept. Because a certain concept or behavior is so popular, we feel we must conform or suffer the consequences of nonconformity. Not so! This attitude suggests there are only two possibilities: conform or suffer. The comfort zone of current culture can be very difficult to break out of because to do so we are in a very small minority, and this can feel very risky and frightening. This fear can be eradicated by a full understanding of the nature of reality as limitless energy and non-finite possibilities. Conformity to the beliefs of current culture is not implicitly necessary. We must be the brave instigators of a root paradigm shift and lead by example.

Chapter Five: Helpful Tips

1. A firm decision/commitment to the new paradigm must be made. You must make up your mind! An irrevocable decision for change must be made. This decision must be for a total transformation of mind and being. Your comfort zone must become unacceptable to you. A commitment to this transformation must follow, and your life must become saturated with new beliefs which are based on the true nature of reality and your relationship to it until this new paradigm becomes your new conditioning.

2. Belief in possibilities is essential. You must retrain your mind to be focused on possibilities and not on the finite evidence of your senses. Keep in mind that the intelligence of the field of potentialities is far beyond anything the mind can comprehend. This intelligence knows how to orchestrate the outcomes of your thoughts and beliefs in ways that you cannot imagine. This is the origin of miracles. It is much easier to believe in, and stay focused on infinite potentialities if you don't feel that the only possibilities available to you are the ones that you yourself can figure out how to actualize.

3. Congruence of belief and behavior is essential. This critical tip is spelled out in missing link number four in the previous chapter, but it is so important that it is worth mentioning again here. Focus and follow through on aligning your behavior with your new beliefs. This especially includes *ceasing to behave in accordance with limiting beliefs from the old paradigm*.

4. Observe feelings, speech, and behaviors as clues to beliefs. While our entire lives, and especially our relationships, are outward reflections of our inner belief systems, our feelings, speech and behaviors in particular can provide quick and direct access to the beliefs that are running our lives. Our feelings, speech, and behaviors are very accurate pointers to the hidden beliefs we harbor. Generally speaking, behind negative emotion is a limiting, unsupportive, or erroneous belief. Thoughts and beliefs cause emotions. When you are feeling badly, trace the feeling back and you will usually find a negative or limiting thought or belief behind it. Once discovered, let it go and exchange it for a new expansive thought. Thoughts are possibilities and all possibilities are available to you. Be aware of your speech. Your speech, audible and inaudible, will reveal a great deal about what you truly believe. Your speech is like an ongoing affirmation of what you really believe is true. Observe your behaviors, as what you do follows from what you think. Your behavior is based upon what you believe to be true. You must become aware of your motivations as these will reveal your limiting beliefs. Are your behaviors motivated by fear or scarcity? Then you must believe in a finite and limited material universe, or you may believe that you are a tiny powerless fragment, or some such other erroneous and fear-inducing belief.

5. Helpful wording of affirmations. Many people use affirmations to assist them in updating their beliefs, though quite often there is a conflict between the positive statement of the new belief and how they really feel inside. Their newly stated belief is unbelievable to them. As formerly explained, it is easier to believe in new beliefs if the true nature of reality is understood; i.e. that the true nature of reality is a non-finite field of potentialities awaiting the choice of our thought to bring possibilities into five sense or "material" manifestation. *Beliefs and thoughts are simply possibilities*, there for the choosing. As such, I have found that wording affirmations according to the following examples helps the mind to more easily accept the new belief:

~There exists a potential in which my self image is *completely* positive; a potential in which my self view has undergone a 180 degree transformation and the metamorphosis is *unmistakable*! I realize that potential right now.

~Because I am now open to possibilities, money comes to me in many different ways, from many different sources. I put no limits on the ways and means money can come to me.

~There exists a potential in which my new business venture is truly helpful for millions of people and I claim that potential *now*.

~There exists a potential in which I experience sufficiency of supply and I claim that potential now!

~Right now, there exists a potential in which the perfect title for my book exists. I claim that potential *now*.

~Right now there exists a potential in which I have total clarity and inspiration about the vocation which best suits me and best serves others. I claim that possibility now.

6. Use a variety of reprogramming tools to saturate the mind with new beliefs. I recommend using a variety of tools for the reprogramming and transformation of your mind. The key is to saturate your mind with the new belief system. A variety of methods makes this process more effective because no single method becomes redundant, boring, and unimpressive to the mind. Some well-known techniques include: making your own tailor-made videos which include relevant and uplifting images, affirmations, and inspiring music; making affirmation cards and placing them around your living spaces (move them around frequently so they don't become an unnoticed part of the background); reading books and articles; watching videos; and listening to uplifting and inspiring music . You can add guided meditations, video or audio of affirmations, and visualizations of your own imagination. Another potentially helpful tool is to record yourself as if you were enthusiastically speaking to a friend about your transformation or the achievement of your new expanded reality as if it were happening in the present tense. Play it back and listen to it. It can be very empowering. The idea here is to use many varied tools of transformation in a concentrated fashion in order to promote a total transformation of your belief system.

Epilogue

The information contained in this little book is not necessarily new but it is presented in some new ways that may be helpful for understanding and applying its content. It is the result of copious amounts of research, trial and error, flashes of intuitive insight, and inner guidance. The content is intended to be a distillation of information from many sources down to the essential knowledge necessary for a transformation of mind, and the effective conscious creation of experience. It is meant to be a primer for understanding the nature of reality and our relationship to it, and a practical handbook for upgrading our belief systems and our lives. The use of the tree metaphor makes the basic content easy to remember, and the subconscious mind responds particularly well to images.

Before we part, I want to stress one more time that

in order for the conscious creation of experience to be successful, it is essential that your behavior is aligned with your upgraded beliefs. You may have heard that what you do comes from what you think, or that thought produces feelings and these in turn inform your behavior. That is correct. However, many people, despite practicing thought and belief updating techniques for a portion of their day, engage in actions and behaviors based on their old paradigm for the remainder of the day. This implies that they *truly* believe in the old limited paradigm. What they are doing *is* coming from what they are thinking. And what they are thinking and believing is old limited beliefs. The behavior *reveals* the belief. Since the infinite field of potentiality responds to our thoughts and beliefs, it will respond to these limiting beliefs revealed and affirmed by our behavior. If you say or affirm you believe one thing but your behavior reveals that you believe it's opposite, then those conflicting beliefs will neutralize each other, or the more strongly held belief will prevail. This causes either no outer change, or minimal change at best.

The difficulty many people experience in aligning their behavior with their upgraded beliefs shows up especially strongly with regard to money and supply. Their old, strongly programmed beliefs in lack and limitation cause fear and anxiety, frightening them into loyalty to their old behaviors with regard money and supply. Scarcity-based behaviors take the forms of deprivation, of attempting to minimize loss, and of trying to hold on tightly to what one has. These behaviors betray one's mistaken belief in the inert and finite nature of reality. The nature of reality is *not finite*. Therefore, I think, feel and behave accordingly. Money comes and goes and circulates in an ever-revolving cycle from an inexhaustible well of supply.

It is my sincere wish that as a result of your exposure to The Tree of Beliefs that you experience a sense of expansion, both in your mind and in your life.

****

Thank you for taking time to read The Tree of Beliefs. If you found it helpful, please consider telling your friends or posting a review. Word of mouth is an author's best friend and much appreciated.

JO-ELLEN FICO

ABOUT THE AUTHOR
(Official Bio)

Jo-Ellen Fico has devoted her life to the study and application of the transformation of mind and the art of consciously creating experience. Her passion to uncover the true nature of reality and our relationship to it has been the guiding theme of her life. Along her journey she received a Bachelor of Science degree in Applied Mathematics and Management Science from Carnegie-Mellon University, a Bachelor of Arts degree in Music from SUNY Stony Brook where she graduated summa cum laude, a Master of Music degree in Piano Performance from California State University Long Beach where upon graduation she was granted the Graduate Dean's List Award for University Scholars and Artists, and in 2003 she earned a Master of Arts degree in Spiritual Psychology from the University of Santa Monica. Jo-Ellen is a mandala artist, a classical pianist, and she currently mentors people in spiritual psychology and the mechanics of conscious creation. She lives, writes, and frolics in Hawaii.

(Unofficial Bio from the Heart)

Free thinker, "red pill" pusher, mad about mandalas, unabashedly dances in the street.

Made in the USA
Middletown, DE
05 April 2021